DATE DUE

APR 3 0 1975			

Let's Pretend
It Happened
to You

Let's Pretend
It Happened
to You

A Real-People and Storybook-People
Approach to Creative Dramatics

Bernice Wells Carlson

Illustrated by Ralph J. McDonald

ABINGDON PRESS Nashville · New York

LET'S PRETEND IT HAPPENED TO YOU

Copyright © 1973 by Abingdon Press

Library of Congress Cataloging in Publication Data

CARLSON, BERNICE (WELLS) Let's pretend it happened
to you.
Summary: Presents eleven folk tales with directions for
organizing dramatic improvisations of each story.
Bibliography: p.
1. Children's plays—Presentation, etc. 2. Improvisation
(Acting) [1. Plays—Improvisation. 2. Folklore]
I. Title.

　　　　PN3157.C28　　　　792'.028　　　　73-1488

ISBN 0-687-21503-X

MANUFACTURED BY THE PARTHENON PRESS AT
NASHVILLE, TENNESSEE, UNITED STATES OF AMERICA

In memory of my brother,
George Byron Wells, Jr.,
and
in appreciation of
his efforts to help children and youth
develop sensitivity to
the basic humanity in all people

Acknowledgments

I should like to thank the many boys and girls who helped me prepare this book over a period of years—children in public schools, in church-related programs, in library storytelling groups, in summer recreation activities, in a residential camp, in a preschool program, and in Brownie Girl Scouts, and most of all my own two children, Christine and Philip, and my grandchildren, Nancy, David, and Robert Umberger.

I should like to thank also the librarians and teachers who offered professional advice, especially Marie Wilt, a teacher in the Cranford, New Jersey, public schools; and also the people who helped me find, and in some cases translate, appropriate tales from other lands, especially Yoshiko Yokoshi Samuel, Yellow Springs, Ohio; Abraham Halprin, Hallandale, Florida; Melanie Kryvokulsky, Elizabeth, New Jersey; Mrs. Azardikt Shahabi, Tehran, Iran; Sarah Gordon, Highland Park, New Jersey; and Lois Howe, Somerset, New Jersey.

Contents

Let's Pretend
It Happened
to You

Books by Bernice Wells Carlson

Act It Out
Do It Yourself—Tricks, Stunts, and Skits
Fun for One—or Two
The Junior Party Book
Listen! And Help Tell the Story
Make It and Use It
Make It Yourself
The Party Book for Boys and Girls
Play a Part
The Right Play for You
You Know What? I Like Animals

Bernice Wells Carlson with David R. Ginglend
Play Activities for the Retarded Child
Recreation for Retarded Teenagers
and Young Adults

Bernice Wells Carlson with Kari Hunt
Masks and Mask Makers

Bernice Wells Carlson with Ristiina Wigg
We Want Sunshine in Our Houses

Introduction

What Are "Let's-pretend-it-happened-to-you" Dramatics?

"Let's pretend it happened to you is the key to creative dramatics, an activity that prompts a person to put himself in another's shoes, and thus encourages the understanding of other people. In order to create a scene from a real-life or storybook situation, each actor must imagine that, for a brief time, he really is another person. In order to do this, he must try to feel like another person, think like another person, and then walk and talk like another person. Only then can he hope to act like another person.

The jump from being one's self to being another person can never be abrupt. A child realizes gradually that the people around him, and the characters in a story, are a lot like him. Like other real people, and like storybook people, a child is sometimes lazy, surprised, happy, bothered, uncomfortable, bewildered, silly, or smart. Often events that happen in a story of long ago or faraway are similar in essence to things that can happen to a child and his family and friends today.

Storybook people, here-and-now people, and people everywhere in the world have problems, joys, and experiences that make them laugh or cry or fear or hate or love. Sometimes characters and real people use their wits and act bravely. Sometimes they are silly or cowardly. When a child acts out a here-and-now situation or a storybook situation, he learns a little about the universality of human nature and emotions.

Creative dramatics is an elastic term which, in general, means acting out a situation without set lines and with no thought of future production. For most children, it starts with playing cowboys or house and—with encouragement—may advance to acting out stories known to everyone in a group.

This book differs from other books on creative dramatics because it stresses the relationship between real-life people and storybook people. Each dramatic project starts with a game, a pantomime, or some other activity, or with acting out a real-life situation that is related in some way to the story that follows.

A group of children may be asked, "Do you think you could disguise your voice if you had to?" They may play a "Guess-who?" game in an effort to find out. Or perhaps they are asked: "How would you feel if you suddenly saw something you hadn't expected to see? How would you show your feeling?" They may then play a pantomime game.

Or they may be given a real-life situation and asked: "What would you do if this happened to you? How would you feel?" They think about it, talk about it, and then act it out—sometimes with different endings.

The children then listen to the story, trying to "feel" like the characters in it. After the story they discuss the characters, recall the story line, and, after a bit of planning, act out part or all of the tale.

INTRODUCTION

With this method, children move from the familiar to the new. It is hoped that children who take part in this type of creative dramatics will come to realize that any story that deals honestly with human emotions is relevant to their own lives. It is hoped also that each child will gain the ability to put himself in the position of another person and thereby eventually develop sensitivity toward all people.

Unfortunately, most creative dramatics programs sponsored by schools and other public organizations start with third graders. Frequently the emphasis is on acting with the idea of an eventual performance. Much younger children can enjoy, and benefit from, directed creative dramatics when there are no plans for production.

The material in this book is for children of preschool age through the early grades, although the basic method can be used with older children. The entire accent here is on encouraging a child to feel and express his feelings, to work with other children, and to act within the framework of loosely given instructions. With repeated pleasurable experiences, a child may also learn, without coaching, to analyze a situation, to think on his feet, to speak clearly, to move with grace, and to pay attention to a leader.

The material can be used in any type of appropriate program with no thought of progression toward formal dramatics. It can provide fun for children as they act out a scene and then a story at a Brownie or Cub Scout meeting, in a classroom, at a private party, while waiting for their parents who are attending church, or whenever children want to do something different. The leader may be any interested, outgoing, sensitive adult with or without technical training.

Creative dramatics are sometimes offered as a special program under the sponsorship of a neighborhood house, a library, a Y, or some other organization. Some schools employ creative dramatics specialists who come into the classroom much as music, art, and physical education directors do. The material in this book may be included in any of the above programs. A bibliography at the end of the book lists additional materials that will help any kind of leader.

If a group decides to develop its acted-out story into a play with formalized action and set dialogue, their activity is no longer creative dramatics. The actors, however, may be following a creative approach to formal dramatics, a valuable but different experience.

How to Present "Let's-pretend-it-happened-to-you" Dramatics to Children

The success of any creative dramatics program, no matter how short or how simple, depends to a large extent on the planning that goes into it. Planning starts with the choice of a story and ends with some type of evaluation of the project.

Choosing a tale. Stories and related activities in this book represent a start for a program. Leaders will choose stories to share with their groups because they like the tales and because they think the children in their groups will enjoy acting them out.

Leaders wanting to use other stories will discover that not every tale lends itself to creative dramatics and most stories need cutting. Some stories suitable for other types of creative dramatics do not lend themselves to the "let's-pretend-it-happened-to-you" approach because they involve situations remote from the experience of the average young child.

In choosing a story for "let's-pretend-it-happened-to-you" creative dramatics, look for stories with these elements: a situation related in some way to children's experience; a theme children understand; a manner of telling that both the children and the leader enjoy; a definite story line; dramatic action; strong characterization; simple dialogue; expressed emotions; and an idea and ideal worth remembering.

After choosing a story with all these elements, read it out loud. Cut long descriptive passages and explanations that slow down the story line, being careful to preserve the flavor and spirit of the tale.

Choose a preliminary activity or real-life situation related to the tale, taking a cue from activities in this book.

Introducing the activity. A few guidelines may help a leader to introduce a let's-pretend-it-happened-to-you project.

1. Get and hold the attention of everyone. Demand self-discipline.

2. Be enthusiastic about the project.

3. Explain clearly what the group will do.

4. Proceed with sensitivity.

5. Praise everyone who earnestly tries to do anything well.

6. Keep the activity fun.

A favorable physical setup may help a leader get and hold the attention of the group. If the group is small, have them sit in a circle or around a table, so that the leader can see every face and the children can look at the leader and at each other. If the group is larger, stand before it. Allow no distraction—nothing in the children's hands, no children squeezed together. If children must remain at desks, all the desks should be cleared.

From this point on, the leader proceeds in accordance with the background, age, and experience of the children, and the nature of the program in which they are working. Children who have had experiences with creative rhythmic interpretive dancing, pantomime, and informal puppet plays usually respond quickly to other types of creative dramatics. Children with less experience may need to be coaxed and encouraged, little by little, to pretend they are someone else or that they themselves are in a new situation.

Opening activity. One way to start an activity is to have the children do something together that will establish the importance of a cue and help them develop the ability to stop and pay attention. For example, ask everyone to clap until he sees the leader raise one hand, then stop. From then on, the raised hand is a signal to stop. Or choose a simple activity related to the story. For example, if the story is about a lazy elf, say, "Let's all yawn. Stop when I raise my hand."

The leader then introduces the game or real-life situation. For a game, any of several methods may be used to choose quickly who will be IT. For a real-life situation, the director explains the setup and asks for volunteers. If several volunteer for one part, the director says, "We'll act it out more than once." The situation is kept informal and enjoyable with no big to-do about who will play what.

If there are no volunteers, the leader may say, "I'll be a lazy boy. Who will try to wake me up?" (or whatever the situation may call for). Then, "Who else can be a lazy boy?"

INTRODUCTION

After the preliminary activity comes the story.

Reading the story. The leader makes a few remarks about the tale and urges the children to try to "feel" like the characters. A few guidelines may help the leader to read effectively.

1. Know the story well enough that you are able to read it with expression, glancing only now and then at the book.

2. Emphasize the dramatic portions by reading them slowly, with practiced timing, and in such a manner that the children feel that they are there, taking part in an event.

3. In reading dialogue, exaggerate the differences in speech patterns. The children must be able to identify each character as an individual person. A different tone of voice, or pitch, or rate of speaking will help to make each character stand out.

4. Portray emotions with your voice and facial expressions.

5. Continue to use the book, even if you know the tale by heart. One aim of the program is to help children realize that characters in a well-written story are very much like themselves and like people they know.

Story discussion and play planning. At the end of the story discuss it briefly with the children, letting them give their initial reactions. Then concentrate on the dramatization.

A leader may choose either to dramatize only one scene from the story, or to have the children act out the entire tale. In either event, discuss the people in the scene.

"What kind of person was Hans (or any other character)?"
"Brave."

"We need a brave person to be Hans." (Avoid using the expression "to play" Hans.) "Who would like to be Hans?" Choose someone quickly. Don't have tryouts. If two children insist on being Hans, say, "We'll play the scene two times." And be sure to do so. If necessary, choose characters by drawing lots, or by some other impartial method. Use good judgment and don't let the choosing of characters turn into a major project or a popularity contest. Don't let the children argue. Get on with the acting.

If a girl wants to play a boy's part, let her. (Boys seldom want to play girls' parts.) If when it comes to choosing minor parts, a realistic girl does not want to be a farmer and there are no more female parts available, say, "We'll change the story a little. We'll pretend that the farmer's wife, rather than the farmer, was walking down the road." Very often the sex of a minor character in a story is unimportant. For example, it makes little difference whether a traveler meets a man or woman on the road.

If there is a crowd in the story, urge—but don't try to force—everyone to take part. For example, after the main characters have been chosen, a leader might say, "The rest of us will be people in the marketplace. We're *amazed* to see a hippopotamus walking down the street."

If the story has only a few characters and no crowd, or if the group involved is a large one, a number of children will form an audience.

After the characters have been chosen, review the story, making sure that everyone understands the sequence of events. Page through the book during this recall. When the story is well in mind, announce where the action will take place. "This is the road the camel walks down." Pace it off.

"This is the place where the monkey is hiding." The monkey climbs on a chair.

"This is where the dragon is hiding." The dragon crawls under the table.

The scene may be enacted in a designated spot that resembles a stage, or the action may take place all over a room. In any event, no attention is paid to dramatic technique, such as facing the audience. The entire emphasis is on acting like another person, within the framework of the story or scene.

Let's act. This is the point in the creative dramatics program where the sensitivity and ingenuity of the leader shine through. The leader, or director, must urge the most reluctant child to take part without forcing him to do so. The leader must keep the story line moving without seeming to direct the players, and must stir up enthusiasm by example, either as a member of the audience or as a member of the acting group.

In the beginning at least, the leader may want to join the actors in a minor role. As a member of a crowd, the leader may ask a reluctant child a direct question that causes him to respond instinctively: for example, "Did you ever see a hippopotamus in the street before?" Or the leader may take the child's hand and say, "Let's stay close together. I don't know what a hippopotamus might do, do you?" If the child shakes his head, he's starting to act.

If a child forgets when to enter, the leader may prompt him by saying, "I think I see an old man coming down the road," or by giving some other clue that becomes part of the scene.

If the play needs more pep, the director may lead the crowd that yells, as they rush out to meet the king, "Welcome, King! Welcome!"

The leader must not let the questioning or efforts to urge a reluctant child to take part impede the progress of the acting. A few guidelines may help in making decisions about when and how much to become involved in the acting.

1. Keep the story line moving.

2. Keep the structure of the action and the dialogue fluid.

3. Encourage the children to use their own language.

4. If, however, a child seems frustrated and can't remember what a character did or said, tell him.

5. Never correct a child while the story is in progress nor permit another child to do so.

6. Give supportive help when necessary.

Evaluation. At the end of the dramatization, evaluate the acting without criticizing anyone. Praise each child who acted and ask the group, "What was good about his acting?" When answers are complete, ask, "In what way could the acting be better?"

If there is time, and if interest is still keen, replay the scene or the entire story. First ask, "Who would like to play ———?" Name each part and choose the characters quickly. Encourage different children to try. They may like to play the same scene a number of times. Chances are that it will improve each time.

For example, a group of six- and seven-year-olds acted out the scene from *The Talking Cat* where Tante Odette opens the door of her outdoor oven and finds a skunk inside.

The first child opened the imaginary door, held his nose, and yelled, "Skunk!" The children who followed opened the door more slowly and registered increasing horror.

The last volunteer, an all-boy, "he's-bound-to-be-a-football-player" type, had at first appeared to be totally uninterested in the project. At last he picked up a pointer and, using it as a cane, hobbled to the imaginary oven, bent over as if every bone in his body ached. He opened the door a little, poked inside with the stick; he opened the door wide and saw the skunk. With his eyes popping out of his head, he yelled, "A skunk in MY oven!" Then he fainted, lying full length on the floor.[1]

The scene was amazing, because time after time this boy had done no more than passively join a group cheering a knight who had saved a kingdom or gaping at a hippopotamus that had ventured into town.

Not every child, whether obviously endowed or a late bloomer, will be able or willing to show dramatic creativity. But no one can say that a particular child can't or won't *feel* dramatically if he takes part in an activity that constantly emphasizes sensitivity toward and understanding of other people—if the activity is also fun.

---

[1] Natalie Savage Carlson, *The Talking Cat* (Harper & Brothers, 1952).

Wet and Crowded

Let's pretend you are out walking. You feel a drop of rain. The drops come faster and faster. You are getting very wet. You run for shelter. How do you feel? What kind of shelter did you find?

Let's pretend the same thing again. Only this time let's run and find shelter in a very small bus-stop shed. One person arrives, then another, then another, and another. Soon you are all squeezed together. How does it feel to be crowded?

Let's listen to the story "Under One Toadstool." Let's try to imagine that we are the creatures who are wet and crowded. Let's feel as they must feel.

Later we'll act out the story and pretend that it happened to us.

Under One Toadstool

A little ant scurried through the grass that grew near a pond in Russia. It was a beautiful spring day. The sky was bright and the clouds were white. The little ant had much to do.

Suddenly, without a bit of warning, the sky grew dark. A big black cloud appeared. The little ant felt a drop of rain.

"Who's afraid of a drop of rain?" the ant laughed to himself. "Everyone loves a spring shower." He went about his business.

More rain fell, then more and more. Faster and faster came the drops until the little spring shower became a deluge of cold, pounding water. The sky seemed to open up and pour rain down upon the little ant.

"Oh, oh! What shall I do?" cried the bedraggled ant, soaked through and through. "If I stay here, I'll surely drown!"

Looking around, he spied a toadstool that he hadn't
noticed before. It was a very small toadstool. "Maybe if I
crouch down low, I can squeeze under the toadstool and
keep dry," the ant reasoned.

So the ant pulled himself together, crept as close to
the ground as he could, and squeezed himself under the
toadstool.

The toadstool grew just a little.

The ant turned himself around. There in the grass,
near the edge of the pond, stood a bedraggled moth, his
waterlogged wings stuck to his body so that he couldn't
possibly fly.

"Oh, oh! What shall I do?" cried the drenched moth.
"If I stay here, I'll surely drown."

"Come! Come! Creep under the toadstool," urged the
ant.

"There isn't room," wept the moth. "The toadstool's
too small to shelter us both."

"Try! Try!" urged the ant. "We can squeeze together
and both keep dry."

So the moth pulled himself together, crept as close to
the ground as he could, and squeezed himself under the
toadstool.

The ant and the moth were crowded, but they were
dry together under one toadstool.

The toadstool grew just a little.

"Squeak! Squeak!" came a cry. The ant and the moth turned in the direction of the sound. There in the grass, near the edge of the pond, stood a bedraggled field mouse, his wet fur plastered against his skin.

"Oh, oh! What shall I do?" cried the drenched mouse. "If I stay here, I'll surely drown."

"Come! Come! Creep under the toadstool," urged the ant and the moth.

"There isn't room," wept the field mouse. "The toadstool's too small to shelter us all."

"Try! Try!" urged the ant. "We can squeeze together and all keep dry."

So the mouse pulled himself together, crept as close to the ground as he could, and squeezed under the toadstool.

The ant, the moth, and the field mouse were crowded, but they were dry together under one toadstool.

And the toadstool grew just a little.

A pitiful "cheep, cheep," caught the attention of the ant, the moth, and the field mouse. Somehow they managed to turn themselves around in the direction of the sound.

There in the field at the edge of the pond stood a bedraggled sparrow, his feet in a puddle of water and his feathers drooping down.

"Oh, oh! What shall I do?" cried the drenched sparrow. "If I stay here, I'll surely drown."

"Come! Come! Creep under the toadstool," called the ant, the moth, and the field mouse.

"There isn't room," wept the sparrow. "The toadstool's too small to shelter us all."

"Try! Try!" urged the ant. "We can squeeze together and all keep dry."

So the sparrow pulled himself together, crept as close to the ground as he could, and squeezed himself under the toadstool.

The ant, the moth, the field mouse, and the sparrow were crowded, but they were dry under one toadstool.

The toadstool grew just a little.

Suddenly a cry, "Help! Help!" pierced the air. The ant, the moth, the field mouse, and the sparrow turned in the direction of the sound. A rabbit bounded into sight.

"Hide me! Hide me!" yelled the rabbit. "The sly old fox is chasing me. He wants to eat me."

"Come! Come! Creep under the toadstool," called the ant, the moth, the field mouse, and the sparrow.

"There isn't room," cried the rabbit. "The toadstool's too small to shelter us all."

"Try! Try!" urged the ant. "We can squeeze together and hide you."

So the rabbit pulled himself together, crept as close to the ground as he could, and squeezed himself under the toadstool on the side farthest away from the path.

The ant, the moth, the field mouse, the sparrow, and the rabbit were crowded; but they were happy, trying to protect the rabbit under one toadstool.

The toadstool grew just a little.

"Swish-swish—" came the sound of parting grasses as something moved along the path.

"Pad-pad—" came the sound of soft paws touching the earth.

"Sniff-sniff—" came the sound of some creature trying to catch a scent in the rain. A sly old fox appeared.

"Good morning," he said. "Did you see a nice plump rabbit? I was following him down this path, but I lost his scent in the rain. I'd like very much to find that rabbit. Did you see him?"

"Oh, yes, we saw him," said the ant, trying to sound brave. "A rabbit went in that direction," he added, pointing down the path that led away from the toadstool.

"Thank you! Thank you!" said the fox as he slunk away.

There was no sound under the toadstool that sheltered the ant, the moth, the field mouse, the sparrow, and the rabbit. Each creature was too frightened to move until they heard an "Urr-umpf! Urr-umpf!" It was a frog.

"What are you doing crowded together under one toadstool?" he asked the ant, the moth, the field mouse, the sparrow, and the rabbit.

"We are hiding the rabbit from the sly old fox," whispered the ant.

"The fox is gone," croaked the frog.

"We are also keeping dry," explained the sparrow. "We almost drowned in the rain."

"Rain?" croaked the frog. "The rain has stopped." Out from under the toadstool crept the ant, the moth, the field mouse, the sparrow, and the rabbit. "It's stopped, it's stopped. The rain has stopped!" cried all the creatures.

"We are dry!" sang the sparrow.

"No one drowned!" said the moth.

"But how did so many of us get under *one* toadstool?" asked the ant, as he looked around at the moth, the field mouse, the sparrow, the rabbit, and himself.

"Urr-umpf! Urumpf!" croaked the frog. "It was easy. Look at the toadstool. See what happened."

"It grew," said the ant.

"The toadstool grew!" echoed the other creatures.

"Yes, the toadstool grew," agreed the frog. "Just like your hearts."

"Our hearts?" asked the other creatures.

"Yes," said the frog. "Each time you did a friendly act, your hearts grew a little. You became bighearted creatures, under a big toadstool."

"That's a nice idea," said the ant.

"A very nice idea," said the mouse. "I could dance for joy."

"And I could hop," said the rabbit.

"And I could fly," said the moth and then the sparrow.

So round and round the creatures darted, each in his own way, on a spring day in Russia.

—A Russian tale retold

What Noise Was That?

Let's play "What Noise Was That?" One person is Iᴛ. Iᴛ sits in a chair, closes his eyes, and puts his hands over his eyes. Everyone else, including the leader, scatters around the room. The leader, in a whisper, asks someone to make a certain noise: for example, to clap, to knock two blocks together, to snap his fingers, or to make some other noise. Then everyone counts to ten together, out loud, while the leader runs away from the noisemaker.

At the count of ten, Iᴛ opens his eyes. He tries to guess what the noise was and goes to the player who made it. If Iᴛ guesses correctly, the noisemaker becomes Iᴛ. If Iᴛ guesses incorrectly, the leader chooses another player to be Iᴛ.

Now let's pretend that you are daydreaming with your eyes shut tight. You hear a loud noise behind you. How do you feel? What do you do? Let's act it out.

Let's listen to the story about a timid rabbit and find out what he did when he heard a loud noise behind him. Let's try to "feel" like the timid rabbit. Later we'll act out the story.

The Timid Rabbit

Once upon a time, in far-off India, a rabbit sat under a coconut tree. He was daydreaming. He thought, "What if the world broke up? What would happen to me?"

At that moment a monkey dropped a coconut. It fell on the ground, blop! right behind the rabbit.

The rabbit jumped up and yelled, "The world is breaking up." He ran away as fast as he could, without looking back.

A deer saw the running rabbit. He called, "Why are you running so fast?"

"The world is breaking up. Come along!" The deer ran with the rabbit.

They passed a fox. "The world is breaking up. Come along!" they yelled. On they ran, and the fox ran with them.

They passed an elephant. "The world is breaking up. Come along!" they yelled. On they ran, and the elephant ran with them.

On and on they ran through the jungle. Other animals heard their cry and ran with them.

At last the lion saw the animals running and heard their cry, "The world is breaking up."

The lion thought, "There must be some mistake." He ran to the foot of a hill in front of them and roared three times.

The animals stopped running. They knew the voice of the king of beasts. They feared him.

"Why are you running?" asked the lion.

"The world is breaking up, O King," answered the animals.

"Who saw it breaking up?" roared the lion.

"Not I," said the elephant. "Not I." "Not I." "Not I," said another animal, and then another, and then another.

"Who saw the world breaking up?" repeated the lion.

"Ask the rabbit," said the deer timidly.

The lion glared at the rabbit. "Did you see the world breaking up?" he asked.

"Well," said the rabbit. "I didn't exactly see the world breaking up. But I know the world is breaking up."

"How do you know?" asked the lion.

"I heard the world breaking up," answered the rabbit.

"Heard the world breaking up?" roared the lion. "Explain yourself."

"I was sitting under a tree," explained the rabbit. "I

thought, 'What if the world broke up? What would happen to me?' Then I heard a noise. It was the world breaking up. So I ran away."

"In that case," said the lion kindly, "you and I will go back to the place where the world started to break up. We'll see what is the matter."

The lion, the rabbit, the deer, the fox, the elephant, and all the other animals went to the place where the rabbit had been sitting, daydreaming, under a coconut tree. There they saw—a COCONUT!

"Is this where you were sitting?" asked the lion.

"Yes," answered the rabbit.

"Do you see the world breaking up?"

"No," answered the rabbit, looking at the smooth, hard ground.

"What do you see?" asked the lion.

"A coconut," answered the rabbit.

"Now, what do you think you really heard?" asked the lion.

"I guess I really heard the noise of a coconut falling on the ground," said the rabbit slowly.

"You ran away from a fallen coconut," said the lion sternly. "You foolish rabbit!"

"You foolish rabbit," yelled all the other animals.

"Quiet!" yelled the lion. "You other animals followed the foolish rabbit." With that remark, the lion turned and stalked away.

The other animals had nothing more to say. They too walked silently away.

The rabbit sat under the coconut tree to dream a new dream.

—A tale from India retold

Too Much Advice

How do you feel when one person tells you to do something one way; then another person tells you to do it another way?

Let's pretend that it's a day in spring. The weather isn't really warm and it isn't really cold. Grandma looks at the thermometer and says, "Mmm, it's rather chilly. You better wear your coat today." She leaves the room. You put on your coat.

Big sister comes into the room. She looks at you and says, "Why are you wearing that coat? It's spring! I'm not going to wear a coat." She leaves the room. You take off your coat.

Mother comes into the room and says, "My, my! I just stepped outside to get the paper. It's not as warm as you think. You better wear your heavy sweater today." She leaves the room and you put on your sweater.

Dad comes in and says, "Just got the weather report. Might rain today. Better wear your raincoat."

What do you do? How do you feel? Act it out.

Now let's listen to the story of "The Man, the Boy, and the Donkey." Try to imagine how the man and the boy feel when they get a lot of advice. Later we'll act out the story.

The Man, the Boy, and the Donkey

A miller and his son started down a country road leading a donkey that they hoped to sell at a neighboring fair. They had not gone far when they met some girls.

"Look!" said one of the girls. "Aren't those people silly? They're leading a donkey. I'd ride, wouldn't you?"

"You bet!" answered the other girl, as they laughed at the man and the boy walking with a donkey between them.

The man heard what the girls had said. Their suggestion sounded sensible. "Get on the donkey and ride," he said to his son. The boy climbed up on the back of the donkey.

Down the road they went. The boy rode the donkey. The man walked beside them. Soon they met some old men.

"See there!" said one of the old men. "Didn't I tell you? No respect for parents these days. See that boy riding while his poor old father walks. Get down, boy! Let your father ride."

Hearing these words, the miller helped his son get off, and he himself rode. The son walked behind. They had not gone far when they met some women at a well.

"What a selfish old man!" cried one of them. "Riding a donkey while the boy runs behind."

"The boy can hardly keep up with the donkey," said another.

"Perhaps we can both ride," said the miller. He helped his son get up behind him. As they neared the town, they paused at the side of a bridge. A man spoke to them.

"Excuse me," he said, "is that your donkey?"

"Oh, yes," said the agreeable miller. "We are taking him into town to sell him at the fair."

"My goodness!" said the man. "How can that little donkey carry two people? He'll drop dead before you get into town. You can't sell a dead donkey. If you want to get that donkey to the fair and sell him, you had better carry him."

"Maybe you are right," agreed the miller. He and his son got off the donkey. They tied his legs together and hung him on a pole. They put the pole on their shoulders and tried to carry the donkey across the bridge that led to town.

Now the donkey did not like to be carried. He jerked and he lurched. He swung back and forth. At last he jerked the pole off the shoulders of the man and boy and fell into the fast flowing river.

The miller and his son looked at the donkey. There was no way to save him. The donkey was gone forever. Then they looked at each other. "You see," said the miller, "we tried to please everyone; but we pleased no one."

"And we lost our donkey, too," added the boy.

Now act out the story. Use a broom for the donkey. One—or two—persons can ride a broomstick. As you lift the donkey, remember that he is heavy.

—One of Aesop's Fables retold

What Do You See?

Let's pretend that someone opens a door and sees something he hadn't expected to see. He'll pantomime—that is, act without saying a word. He'll open the door, show how he feels, and then do something that will help us guess what he sees.

The leader chooses someone who wants to pantomime and shows him a slip of paper with the name of an object written on it; for example, a baseball bat, a puppy dog, or a monster. If the child cannot read, the leader may whisper in his ear.

The leader may open the imaginary door, or the child may choose to do so himself. He reacts to what he sees, and then does something—for example, swings the bat, pets the dog, or runs from the monster. Wait until the end of the scene before guessing what the actor saw.

Let's listen to the story of "The First Tinsel" and try to imagine how you would feel if you saw a decorated Christmas tree for the first time.

43

The First Tinsel

Frau Schmidt was busy, very busy. She was cleaning house for Christmas; and, when Frau Schmidt cleaned house, she really cleaned. She started with the attic. She picked up her big broom and climbed the stairs. Then she stopped and looked around.

"Cobwebs!" she cried. "Cobwebs again. Those spiders!"

She grasped the broom firmly in both hands and went after the spider webs. Back and forth she swept.

At the first stroke of the broom, the spiders woke up from their winter's nap and began to scurry. They hid under the rafters, between the shingles, and under a chest that was too heavy for one person to move—any place to get out of the way of Frau Schmidt and her broom.

Frau Schmidt continued to sweep. She didn't raise much dust because she had just finished the fall house-

44

cleaning when she decided it was time to start the Christmas housecleaning. At last Frau Schmidt stood still and looked at her work.

"It's good," she sighed. "This year I have banished the spiders."

She went downstairs where the Schmidt children were also cleaning. The girls were scrubbing floors and shining windowpanes. The boys were scouring pots and polishing furniture. Outside, Herr Schmidt was cleaning out the stables in the barn.

There was a special reason why Frau Schmidt, Herr Schmidt, and all the Schmidt children were cleaning frantically just before Christmas. The reason was a legend.

According to the legend, the Christ Child roams the earth each year on Christmas Eve. He visits one home and then another. Wherever he visits, he blesses the home and brings joy. No one knows which homes he will visit on any specific Christmas Eve. So each family prepares for his coming by providing a spotless home for his comfort and by decorating a tree in his honor.

Back to the story of the Schmidt family. Christmas Eve finally came, as Christmas Eve always does, whether we are ready for it or not. The family had a simple supper. Then Herr Schmidt and the boys brought in the Christmas tree and placed it carefully in front of the largest window. The moon shown through the window-pane and lighted the branches of the tree.

"Oh, oh!" sang the children. "It's a beautiful Christmas tree."

"Absolutely perfect," sighed Frau Schmidt.

"The best in the forest," declared Herr Schmidt.

"Nothing's too good for the Christ Child," said Gretchen, the oldest girl.

"You're right. Absolutely right," said Frau Schmidt. "Now it's time to trim the tree."

The children rushed to the pastry cupboard and brought out trays and trays of beautifully decorated cookies. There were angels and stars and wise men and fruits. Each cookie had a little hole in the center at the top, and a string through the hole. The family laughed and sang as they hung the cookies on the tree.

Then, as the children watched, Frau Schmidt went to a big chest and tenderly lifted out a box filled with glass ornaments. Her grandfather had blown the glass and shaped it into delicate ornaments years before. No one but Frau Schmidt and Herr Schmidt touched the beautiful ornaments.

The family looked lovingly at the tree as the moonlight shown through the glass ornaments and lighted up the decorated cookies.

"It's a lovely tree," sighed Frau Schmidt.

"Just right for the Christ Child," added Gretchen.

"It's good to honor the Christ Child at home," observed Herr Schmidt; "but we must also honor him in church."

"Of course! Of course!" sang the children, as they put on their warm wraps. Just as the church bells began to peal, the family filed out of the house and trudged through the snow to attend midnight services at the village church.

Now up in the attic, the spiders were shivering under the rafters and between the shingles.

"Why should I shiver up here between these shingles?" cried one spider. "I'm coming down to my old spot under the rocker."

"Me, too!" "Me, too!" said the other spiders as they came out of hiding.

"Why all this cleaning?" asked one spider.

"And in winter when we should be sleeping?" asked another.

"They're cleaning for Christmas," explained a third spider. "Christmas comes in winter."

"Christmas? What's Christmas?"

"Why should they clean for Christmas?"

"Well, what is Christmas?" the spiders asked each other. No one knew anything about Christmas.

"Let's find out about Christmas," suggested one spider.

"How?" asked the others.

"Let's go downstairs and find out about Christmas."

"No, no!" shivered the others. "Not when Frau Schmidt is swinging her broom!"

"No one is swinging a broom now," said the first spider. "The family has gone out. I saw them from my place between the shingles. When the bells started to ring, they went outdoors. They are walking in the snow."

"We can creep downstairs; and, when no one is looking, we'll find out about Christmas. We'll creep quietly."

"Let's try," said the other. "We'll be very quiet."

When spiders are quiet, they are really quiet, the quietest creatures on earth. These spiders crept down the stair walls and down the stairs, under the loft door, and into the big room.

There they saw the Christmas tree—a most glorious sight! For one brief moment they stood in wonderment. Then, all at once, they rushed to the tree. They wanted to see everything up close. They ran around and around the tree, up and up, then down, and around and up and down, from limb to limb. And everywhere they went they left spider webs! Soon the entire tree was covered with spider webs.

Suddenly the door creaked.

"Frau Schmidt! Look out for her broom!" called one spider.

The spiders scampered—across the floor, under the door, up the stairs, and into the attic.

The person who opened the door was not Frau Schmidt, nor Herr Schmidt, nor any of the children. It was the Christ Child. He had come to bless the home because he knew it was a home filled with love and dedicated to hard work.

The Christ Child looked around the big room. Everything was spotlessly clean for his comfort. He looked at the tree. In the moonlight he saw the cookies, faithfully baked and beautifully decorated. He saw the treasured glass ornaments dangling from the branches. He walked toward the tree and stopped.

"What do I see?" he asked. "Spider webs! Is this last year's tree? Surely Frau Schmidt would not allow a tree to stand a year gathering spider webs."

He drew a deep breath. "This smells like a fresh-cut fir tree." He felt the needles, flat, firm, flexible. Not a needle dropped from a branch.

"It is a fresh tree," he said, "but it's covered with spider webs." He looked closely at the thin strands of webbing. "Spider webs are beautiful, in their way, and in their place. But their place is not on a Christmas tree. A Christmas tree should be a sight of splendor. Only a

miracle could turn this Christmas tree into a sight of splendor, a thing of beauty."

Then a miracle happened. The spider webs on the tree turned into strands of sparkling tinsel. The Christ Child smiled, blessed the home, and left.

You can well imagine the surprise of the Schmidt family when they returned from church and found their tree entwined with strands of sparkling tinsel.

"It's beautiful! It's beautiful!" sang the children.

"What happened?" asked Frau Schmidt.

"The Christ Child came," said Gretchen.

"He performed a miracle," cried the other children.

"A beautiful miracle," sighed Frau Schmidt.

Every year after that, the Schmidt family trimmed the Christmas tree with tinsel. No one, truly no one, ever learned that the strands of glittering tinsel were really spider webs turned into sparkling splendor.

—A tale found in both German and Norse folklore— with slight variations in the story

Quarrelsome Leaders

Let's pretend you are on a playground. The whistle blows and your teacher calls, "Line up!" Two children rush to the head of the line, each wanting to be the leader. What do the two children say? What do they do? Remember that actors never hurt each other, even when they have a duel on stage. What does the teacher say? What do you think she asks the two children to do? Let's act it out.

Let's listen to a story about two woodpeckers. Each wants to be the leader of the birds. Let's imagine how they feel and how the other birds feel.

Who Should Be Leader?

Long ago, in faraway Poland, the birds of the forest decided to choose a leader.

"I'll be leader," shouted a woodpecker. "I have the sharpest bill. I'll be leader."

"No, I'll be leader," yelled another woodpecker. "I have the strongest bill. I'll be leader."

Then the argument began. At first the two birds screamed at each other. Then they began to push each other around. The other birds couldn't stop them.

"Wait," said the first woodpecker, all of a sudden. "This screaming and pushing is silly."

"Of course it is," answered the second woodpecker. "Everyone who wants me to be leader, raise his feathers."

"Not so fast," said the first woodpecker. "Let's have a contest. See that tree?" The second woodpecker nodded. "We'll climb that tree. First to the top can be leader."

"All right," said the second woodpecker. "Let's go."

The other birds looked at each other as if to say, "What a way to choose a leader!" But they didn't interfere.

The woodpeckers stood on opposite sides of the tree, as the other birds gathered around to watch. "One, two, three, go!" everyone yelled together. The woodpeckers started to climb the tree. Up, up they went, little by little, tap- tap- tapping all the way. And would you believe it? They reached the top of the tree at the same time.

"I won!" yelled the first woodpecker. He tapped the head of the other woodpecker with his bill.

"No, I won," screamed the second woodpecker, He tapped the head of the first woodpecker with his bill.

"Who-o-o-o cares?" hooted the old owl who had been watching the fight. "Who-o-o-o cares which one of you won?"

"Who cares?" chirped the other birds.

"If you two woodpeckers can't get along with each other, how can you get along with other birds?"

"How? How?" chirped the other birds.

"If you two woodpeckers can't get along with other birds, how can you be their leader?" the old owl continued.

The two woodpeckers looked sadly at each other. They had to admit a sad fact. Quarrelsome creatures don't make good leaders.

—Retold from a translation of a story in a Polish storybook

Who Are You?

Could you change your voice and sound like another person if you had to do it? Let's try and see.

One person is IT. IT stands or sits with his back to the rest of the group. The leader points to someone in the group, who says, "Hello" in a very different voice.

IT says, "Who are you?"

The voice answers, "A man from Mars," or "Little Bo Peep" or "Silly Dilly" or any name other than his own.

IT tries to guess who is speaking. If he isn't sure of a name, he points to someone. If IT guesses correctly, the person who gave a new name becomes IT. If IT guesses incorrectly, he is IT again. After two wrong choices, IT chooses someone to take his place.

In the story "The Grandmother and the Butternut Squash," the grandmother must try to change her voice for a very good reason. Let's listen to the story and try to imagine how the grandmother feels. Later, we'll act it out.

When you play the part in the story where the grandmother is inside the butternut squash, crouch down until you look something like a ball. Throw a scarf or other cloth over your head, but let your face show enough so that you can see where you are going. Shuffle along, barely lifting your feet, and just pretend that you are rolling. Pretend that you hit a rock. Don't bump into anything and get hurt.

The Grandmother and the Butternut Squash

There was once a grandmother who lived in a village with a mountain behind it. She had a big garden and trees that bore fruit which she often shared with the children who came to visit her.

On the other side of the mountain there was another village, where the grandmother's daughter lived with her husband, who was a chief.

One day the grandmother filled her basket with various fruits and said to the children, "I must go to visit my daughter and my son-in-law. Good-bye. I'll see you when I get back."

The grandmother had not gone far when she met a wolf. The wolf put his paws on his hips, showed his teeth, and growled, "Old woman, the gods have sent you to be my lunch. I want to eat you; so get ready."

The grandmother was frightened at first. Then she

thought, "Fright does no good." She used her brains and said, "Eat *me?* Why do you want to eat *me?* I'm not fat enough. Let me go to the party and get fat. Wait and eat me when I come back."

At first the wolf didn't like the idea. Then he said to himself, "She's right. She's nothing but skin and bones. I'll let her get fat and put meat on her bones. She'll be delicious then."

So he said to the grandmother, "All right. I'll wait until you get fat and come back. I'll eat you then."

The grandmother walked and walked and walked. Halfway up the mountain she met a sleeping tiger who was lying so that one leg and paw made a column holding up his head. As the grandmother neared, he woke up, looked at the grandmother, played with his moustache, and said, "Hmmm! Old woman, sit beside me until I want to eat you. Be ready for me."

The grandmother was not as frightened as she had been when she met the wolf. She said, "Don't eat me now. Let me go to the party and get fat. Then you can eat me."

"All right," agreed the tiger. "I'll sleep a little until you come back. Then I'll eat you."

The grandmother walked on and on. Near the top of the mountain she stopped a moment, wiped her face with the corner of her apron, and laughed, saying to her-

self, "When you get two, you always get three. I think I'll see a lion before I see my daughter and my son-in-law."

She looked around and, sure enough, there was a lion sitting in the shade. He patted the ground three times and growled as gently as a lion can growl, "I was going hunting just now, but I've changed my mind. Come here, grandmother. I'll eat you instead."

The grandmother laughed at the lion and said, "Don't eat me now. I can't fill you up. Let me go to the party and get fat. Then you can eat me."

"All right," said the lion. "I'll get something to eat for a day or two. Then when you come back, I'll eat you."

The grandmother laughed to herself, but said nothing. At last she came to the home of her daughter and her son-in-law. What a happy reunion! Although the grandmother was almost too tired to talk, she told her tale. In fact she told it over and over again during her visit.

After a week, the grandmother said, "You know, children, I must go home."

"You can't go," cried her daughter.

"What about the wolf, the tiger, and the lion?" asked her son-in-law.

"You'll see," answered the grandmother. "Get me a big butternut squash, a squash as large as I am." The son-in-law went to the field and brought back a huge butternut squash, round at the bottom and long at the top. The grandmother cut it in two, and then scooped out all the seeds and meat, leaving only a hollow shell.

The next morning, the grandmother, her daughter, and her son-in-law took the butternut squash to the top of the mountain path. "Now, children," the grandmother said, "it is time to say good-bye. I am going to get inside the butternut squash. I want you to fasten it together and roll me down the mountain path." The daughter and the son-in-law did as the grandmother requested.

The butternut squash rolled and rolled until it came to the lion, who yelled, "Butternut squash, did you see an old woman?"

The grandmother inside the butternut squash changed her voice and answered, "No, I didn't see an old woman. Let me go. Roll me down the mountain."

The lion licked his lips and rolled the butternut squash down the mountain.

The butternut squash rolled and rolled until it came to the tiger. The tiger stopped the butternut squash and asked, "Butternut squash, did you see an old woman?"

The grandmother inside the squash changed her voice and answered, "No, I didn't see an old woman. Let me go. Roll me down the mountain."

The tiger licked his lips and rolled the butternut squash down the mountain.

The butternut squash rolled and rolled until it bumped into the wolf, who was standing in the path waiting for the old woman to come back.

"Butternut squash," growled the wolf, who by this time was very angry, "did you see an old woman?"

The grandmother inside the butternut squash changed her voice and answered, "No, I didn't see an old woman. Let me—"

The wolf recognized the voice of the grandmother at once and yelled, "Old woman, I know you. I'm going to eat you right now."

He rolled the butternut squash against a stone. It split open. Out jumped the old woman. In rushed the wolf, and his head got stuck in the squash.

The grandmother calmly wiped her dress. The wolf howled and howled, his head still stuck in the squash. The grandmother laughed a little and said, "You better run away before I call the people who will come and beat you."

So the wolf ran away with his head still stuck in the butternut squash. The grandmother returned to her garden, where the children were waiting. Together they picked some fruit and then sat down, while the old woman told the most unusual tale of the grandmother and the butternut squash.

—A tale from Iran retold

A Muddy Mess

Let's pretend that you are wearing something new that you want us to see. Hold up one foot if you want us to notice your shoes. Or look at your hands and turn them over and over if you want us to notice your new gloves or mittens. Twirl around to show us the full skirt of a new dress. Button up a new coat or jacket, and turn around slowly so that we can see how grand you look.

Now let's pretend that you are showing off a new dress or suit. As you turn around to show us how grand you look, you lose your balance and fall into a mud puddle. What do you do? How do you feel? Show us by your actions and by the expression on your face.

Now let's listen to the story of "How the Blue Bird and the Coyote Got Their Colors." Try to imagine how they feel. Later we'll act it out.

How the Blue Bird and the Coyote Got Their Colors

Long ago, before man walked on earth, all the birds were an ugly color. Not a shiny black, not a lustrous gray, not a deep brown, and certainly not a bright blue, red, yellow, green, or orange. One, and only one, creature had color—the coyote. He was green.

One day a bird with a beautiful voice and ugly, drab feathers discovered a secret. He went to the lake that no water runs into and no water runs out of. He splashed into the water four times every morning for four mornings. As he splashed he sang a song:

> Tra-lu-da, tra-lu-da!
> O lake that's pure blue,
> Tra-lu-da, tra-lu-da!
> May I be blue too.

After the fourth dip on the fourth morning, something happened. The feathers on the back of the bird turned blue, and the feathers on his breast turned an orange brown. The bird flew over the lake and saw his reflection.

"I'm a blue bird, a blue bird," he sang. He flew into the woods singing over and over again, "I'm a blue bird, a blue bird."

Now the coyote who was green saw the beautiful blue bird and cried out, "Blue bird! Blue bird! Where did you get your pretty coat?"

"In the lake that no water runs into and no water runs out of," sang the bird.

"What did you do?" asked the coyote.

Happily the blue bird told the coyote his secret. He was glad to share his good fortune.

The coyote thought, "I'd like a blue coat. Green is too much like the woods. I'd like to be seen—like the blue bird."

So the coyote went to the lake that no water runs into and no water runs out of. He dipped himself in the water four times every morning for four mornings, and he said the verse that the blue bird had taught him.

> Tra-lu-da, tra-lu-da!
> O lake that's pure blue,
> Tra-lu-da, tra-lu-da!
> May I be blue too!

After the fourth dip on the fourth morning, some-

thing happened. The coat of the coyote turned blue. He looked at his reflection in the lake and he was happy.

Proudly he walked down the forest path, saying, "I've got a blue coat! I've got a blue coat!"

"Where did you get your blue coat?" asked one animal and then another.

"That's my secret," answered the coyote as he walked down the path. "I've got a secret, I've got a secret," he said over and over again. He walked on and on, looking left and right, showing off his coat, paying no attention to the trail.

Suddenly he bumped into a stump. He fell—and landed right in the middle of a mud puddle.

His beautiful blue coat was covered with mud. He brushed his coat to get rid of the mud. He shook his coat to get rid of the mud. He rubbed his coat against the tree trunk. But no matter what that coyote did, he could not get rid of the mud on his coat.

To this very day, the coat of the coyote is a mud-colored brown; and the feathers of the blue bird are blue.

—Based on a Pima Indian tale

What Did You Find?

Let's imagine that we are digging. Who will show us how? Are you digging in sand? Or are you digging in earth? Is the earth dry? Or is the earth wet and gooey?

Let's imagine that you find something. We want to guess what it is. Show us. Maybe you will have to give us some hints. Did a pirate bury it? Did an Indian use it long ago? Did a boy lose it? Are you glad you found it? If we can't guess what it is, you better tell us. Who can dig and find something else?

Let's listen to the story of "Kind Brother, Mean Brother" and imagine how each brother felt when he dug and found something.

Kind Brother, Mean Brother

Long ago, in old Japan, there lived two brothers who were as different as two men could be. The younger brother was a kindly soul who raised chickens for meat and eggs and grew delicious fruits and vegetables, which he shared with the needy, whether man or beast.

The older brother, who lived next door, was as mean as his brother was kind. He worked very little. He cheated when he could. And still he wanted the best of everything for himself. Somehow he managed to eat very well and to live very well, but he shared nothing with the needy, whether man or beast.

One stormy night when the wind was howling and the rain was beating against the house, Mean Brother heard a pitiful barking right outside his door. He ignored the wailing and went on eating his big supper. The barking grew louder and louder.

At last, Mean Brother got up in a huff, stomped across

the mat on the floor, opened the screen, and yelled, "Be quiet! Go away!"

Poor Dog, who was thoroughly wet and shivering, looked up with pleading eyes and whimpered in his most gentle tones. Who could refuse such a gentle dog?

Mean Brother could. He closed the screen, yelling, "Be gone! Be gone! You've spoiled my supper. Be gone!"

Dog limped next door where Kind Brother was also eating supper. His meal was chicken soup, with very little chicken and very little rice in it. For, as usual, Kind Brother had given the best part of the chicken to a needy person, this time a weak grandmother who needed nourishment in order to gain strength.

Again Dog wailed, and Kind Brother listened. "Sounds like a dog," he said to himself. "A wet dog, I'm willing to bet." He got up, crossed the room, and pulled aside the door. "Poor Dog," he said, "come into my house." Dog entered, shivering and dripping wet.

"Poor Dog," repeated Kind Brother, as he tried to dry Dog, "where do you live? Never mind. You can show me tomorrow. How long have you been gone from home? A long time, I know, because you are very thin. Here, drink my soup. You need it more than I do." Kind Brother gave Dog the rest of his soup.

Soon Kind Brother unrolled his mattress, which was his bed. Dog and Kind Brother lay down to sleep until the first ray of dawn broke in the sky.

Dog woke up with a start. He tugged on the jacket of Kind Brother. "Oh," yawned Kind Brother, "I know I should get up and work. Morning is the best time for work. But first play with me, Dog."

Dog pulled on the jacket of Kind Brother. He ran to the door, then back to Kind Brother.

"You want me to follow you, don't you, Dog? All right, I'll take you back to your master. But if you ever want a new home, come live with me."

Down the road they traveled in the early morning, man and dog, slushing through the mud left by the all-night rain. At last Dog stopped in front of a deserted house.

"Is this where you used to live?" asked Kind Brother. "Well, your master has been gone a long time. I bet I know what happened," Kind Brother said, reaching down to pet Dog. "You waited and waited for the family to come back. At last you gave up and went to look for a new home. Well, you can live with me, Dog. Now, let's go back. We have work to do."

Dog did not want Kind Brother to go back. He ran to a spot in the garden. Then he ran to a toolshed. Then he ran back to a spot in the garden. Then he tugged at the pants of Kind Brother.

"All right, I'll follow you," said Kind Brother. In the toolshed Kind Brother found a spade. Dog returned to the spot in the garden. Kind Brother followed and began to dig and dig where Dog pointed. He dug and dug. At last his spade struck some metal. He dug a little more and uncovered a box. He knelt down and lifted it out gently.

He opened it. Inside the metal box was a wooden box. Inside the wooden box was a silk bag. Inside the silk bag were coins—many, many coins.

"A treasure," shouted Kind Brother. "Dog, you helped me find a treasure. Thank you, Dog. Come, let's take it home."

While Kind Brother and Dog were away, Mean Brother had come to the home of Kind Brother to beg or steal vegetables and fruit, as was his custom. He noticed that the house was empty and no one was in sight. He picked the best fruit and vegetables and said, "Where did my brother go today? Lazy lout! I bet he went off with that stray dog. Why should he take a day off to travel with a dog? I might as well rest until he gets back." So saying, Mean Brother went behind a screen and lay down on some pillows.

At last Kind Brother and Dog returned. "I guess we better count this money," said Kind Brother, as he laid the metal box on the table. He opened the metal box, took out the wooden box, and then took out the silk bag.

Mean Brother jumped out from behind the screen. "Where did you get that money?" he screamed. Kind Brother explained that Dog had led him to the spot where the treasure had been buried.

"Find me a treasure," yelled Mean Brother. "If you don't, I'll beat you." He raised his arm as if to strike Dog.

"Don't you dare strike Dog!" yelled Kind Brother, as he stepped between Dog and Mean Brother.

Dog showed no desire to fight. He pulled on a pant leg of Mean Brother and then ran to the door.

"He wants me to follow him," said Mean Brother. "Wait, I'll get my spade. Oh, I forgot, it's broken. I'll use your spade." So picking up his brother's spade, Mean Brother left the house and followed Dog down the muddy road.

"I want you to show me lots of treasure," he said to Dog. "I'm more clever than my brother, so I should have more treasure. My stupid brother works and works —and then gives things away. He's probably working now."

But Kind Brother was not working. He put the coins in the silk bag. He put the silk bag in the wooden box. He put the wooden box in the metal box. He closed the metal box. He picked it up and hurried down the road after Mean Brother and Dog. He wanted to make sure that Mean Brother did not harm Dog or come back to steal the treasure.

Once again Dog led the way to the deserted house. Once again he went to a place in the garden. This time Dog chose a very low spot where the mud was especially gooey. The grass around the edge of the garden was now quite dry.

Mean Brother stepped into the mushy mud and began to dig where Dog pointed. Kind Brother stood on the dry grass and watched. Soon Dog joined Kind Brother and together they watched Mean Brother dig and dig. Each spade of mud was heavy, but Mean Brother did not mind. He was looking for free treasure. At last he struck metal. He shouted with delight. He leaned down to pick it up. But it was trash. He dug again—more trash. And again—more trash. More *trash!* More *trash!* More *trash!*

"I'll get you!" yelled Mean Brother, as he raised his spade.

"No, you won't," shouted Kind Brother. "Dog and I are off to make a new life in a new place. May you have a nice, mean time with your trash and mud."

Off went Dog and Kind Brother, leaving Mean Brother stuck in the mud and trash.

—Based on an old Japanese tale

Something to Carry

Let's each think of something to carry. Don't tell anyone what it is, just think about it. Is it big, or is it little? Is it heavy, or is it light? How will you pick it up? Will you carry it in one hand or in two hands? Or will you carry it on your back or in your arms or on your head? Or will you put it in a wagon and pull it, or in a wheelbarrow and push it?

Who will pantomime? Pretend to pick up the thing you've thought of and then carry it. We'll try to guess what it is.

Now let's pretend that you pick up something and eat it or chew it. We'll try to guess what it is.

Now let's imagine that it is a very hot day. You buy four ice-cream cones. You try to carry them to a picnic table where your family is sitting, but your path is blocked because a playground parade is going by. You are standing there trying to hold the four cones. The cones are melting. How do you feel? What do you do? Let's act out the scene.

Let's listen to "Joseph Francis Remembers." How does the little boy feel as he tries to carry several things in different ways? How does his mother feel when she sees the various things he brings home? After the story, we'll act it out, one scene at a time. Then we'll act out the entire story.

Joseph Francis Remembers

Joseph Francis lived down south, more than fifty years ago, in a little house on a country road. Almost every day he went to visit his auntie, who lived on the same country road, quite a piece away. Very often she gave him something to carry home to his mother.

One day she gave him a big piece of rich, yellow cake.

"Thank you," said Joseph Francis, as he took the rich, yellow cake and said good-bye to his auntie.

Outside the door, Joseph Francis squeezed the cake extra hard in his fist. He didn't want to drop the rich, yellow cake. Then he went along home.

"What's that?" asked his mother when she saw Joseph Francis carrying something in his fist.

"Cake," answered Joseph Francis, "rich, yellow cake." But when he opened his fist, he was holding nothing but crumbs.

"Oh, Joseph Francis," said his mother, "that's no way to carry cake. The way to carry cake is to wrap it up, put it in your hat, and put your hat on your head. Then come along home wtih your head held up. Remember that!"

"I'll remember," promised Joseph Francis.

The next time Joseph Francis visited his auntie, she gave him butter—sweet, fresh-churned butter—to carry home to his mother.

"Thank you," said Joseph Francis, as he took the sweet, fresh-churned butter and said good-bye to his auntie.

Outside the door Joseph Francis remembered what his mother had told him. He wrapped up the butter, put it in his hat, and put his hat on his head. He held his head up high and went along home.

The day was hot—very hot. Soon the butter began to melt. It melted and it melted, and as it melted it ran all over Joseph Francis—over his forehead, into his eyes, over his nose, into his mouth, down his neck. Down, down ran the butter. All the butter Joseph Francis had when he got home was *on* him.

"My goodness!" said his mother, when she looked at Joseph Francis. "What's that all over you?"

"Butter," said Joseph Francis, "sweet, fresh-churned butter."

"Oh, Joseph Francis," sighed his mother, as she tried to get the butter out of his hat, out of his hair, out of his ears, and off his face and neck—off all of him.

"That's no way to carry butter," she told him. "The way to carry butter is to wrap it up in nice green leaves. Take it to the brook and cool it. Cool it, cool it. Then take it carefully in your hands and come along home. Remember that!"

"I'll remember," promised Joseph Francis.

Another day when Joseph Francis visited his auntie, she gave him a little, new puppy dog to carry home to his mother.

"Thank you," said Joseph Francis, as he took the little, new puppy dog and said good-bye to his auntie.

Outside the door he remembered what his mother had told him. He wrapped the puppy dog in nice green leaves. Then he took it to the brook and cooled it. Cooled it, cooled it. The little new puppy dog didn't wiggle much anymore. So Joseph Francis held it carefully in his hands and went along home.

"What's that?" asked his mother, when she saw he was carrying something.

"A puppy dog," answered Joseph Francis, "a little, new puppy dog."

"My goodness!" said his mother, as she took the shivering, little new puppy dog and began to rub him and rub him until he was dry and frisky again.

"Oh, Joseph Francis," sighed his mother. "That's no way to bring home a little, new puppy dog. The way to bring home a little new puppy dog is to put a string around his neck and put him on the ground. Then take hold of the other end of the string and come along home. Remember that!"

"I'll remember," promised Joseph Francis.

Next time Joseph Francis went to visit his auntie she gave him a loaf of light, fresh-baked bread to carry home to his mother.

"Thank you," said Joseph Francis, as he took the loaf of light, fresh-baked bread and said good-bye to his auntie.

Outside the door he remembered what his mother had told him. He tied a string around the loaf, set the loaf on the ground, took the other end of the string, and went along home.

"My goodness!" said his mother, when she saw him coming. "What's that at the end of a string?"

"Bread," said Joseph Francis, "light, fresh-baked bread." "Bread?" said his mother, as she picked up some of the mess from the ground.

"Oh, Joseph Francis," she sighed, "you better not carry things till you're bigger. You go out to play. But let me tell you something. Do you see those six mince pies I baked? Do you see that I set them on the back step to cool? Now you be careful about stepping on those pies. Remember that!"

"I'll remember. I'll be careful," promised Joseph Francis.

His mother put on her shawl, picked up her basket, and went to visit Joseph Francis' auntie.

Joseph Francis looked at the six pies cooling on the back step.

"I'll be careful about stepping on those pies, just like Mother said," he thought. And Joseph Francis *was* careful about stepping on those pies. He stepped carefully —right in the middle of every one!

—Retold from *Epaminondas and His Auntie* by Sara Cone Bryant

Something Special

Let's pretend that you have something you like very much. It may be something to wear, a toy, a pet—or anything. Now think about something you like; but don't say a word.

In order to show what it is we like, we are going to pantomime —that is, act without using words. The leader pretends to pick up something and then pretends to do something with it. Don't guess what it is until the act is finished. Then raise your hands and guess in turn what the leader likes.

Who else will pretend to pick up something that he likes and do something with it? Be sure to show by the expression on your face and the way you handle it how much you like it.

Now let's listen to the story of "The One and Only Cap." Try to imagine how you would feel if you had a cap you really wanted to keep, but you were offered some things that you also would like to have in trade for the cap.

The One and Only Cap

Anders had a new cap. It was a one and only cap. No other cap in the whole world was quite like it. His mother had knitted it just for him. Anders had watched her take a scrap of yellow yarn, a scrap of blue yarn, a scrap of red yarn, and a scrap of green yarn and knit them into a woolly stocking cap with a pretty pattern in the middle and a big blue tassel on top.

When it was finished, his mother had said, "Here is your cap, Anders. I do believe it's a one and only cap. No other cap in the world is just like it. I knitted it just for you."

Anders looked at the cap. It was pretty. He put the cap on his head. It fit perfectly. He pulled it down over his ears. It would be warm in winter, he knew. Then Anders ran to the mirror to make sure that he really did look splendid in his new cap.

"That," said his mother beaming, "is the prettiest cap in Sweden."

"It's the prettiest cap in the world," answered Anders. "Thank you, Mother. Thank you! I just love my one and only cap. I want the whole world to see my cap." Out the door he ran.

"Which way shall I go?" Anders asked himself. "To Grandmother's house? She'd love to see my one and only cap. No, to town. I want lots and lots of people to see my one and only cap that Mother knitted just for me." Down the road he started.

Before long he met a farmer boy walking down the path, whistling as he drove his cows before him.

"Wow!" said the farmer boy, "that's a beautiful cap!"

"It's a one and only cap," explained Anders. "My mother knitted it just for me."

"I wish I had a cap like that," said the farmer boy.

"No other cap in the world is just like it," answered Anders. "It's a one and only cap and I love it."

The farm boy looked serious. He put his hand into his pocket and slowly pulled out a bright and shiny jackknife.

"I'll trade my jackknife for your cap," offered the boy.

Anders had always wanted a jackknife. Even his biggest brother didn't have a fine and shiny jackknife like the one the boy held in his hand. Anders felt his cap. Then he lowered his hands.

"I'd love to have a jackknife," he explained. "But I

90

can't give up my one and only cap that Mother knitted just for me."

Saying good-bye, Anders started down the road again. He passed two fields and soon came to the gate of a little cottage where an old woman stood trimming her hedge. She stood up straight, looked at Anders, and said, "My goodness! What a beautiful cap."

"Thank you," said Anders. "It's a one and only cap. Mother knitted it just for me."

"Did she indeed?" sighed the woman. "It's a splendid cap. Not even the King of Sweden has a cap like that."

"Do you think that's true?" asked Anders.

"I really think it's true," answered the old woman.

"Then maybe I'll show the King my one and only cap, the cap that Mother knitted just for me. Thanks for the suggestion, and good-bye."

Down the road Anders traveled until he came to the gates of the castle. A soldier in uniform guarded the big iron gates. Anders had never seen iron gates or a man in uniform. Suddenly Anders felt small and afraid. Then he thought of his cap and how splendid he looked. He stood up straight and spoke clearly and politely.

"Please, sir, I'd like to see the King."

The guard leaned down and said, firmly but kindly, "I am sorry, sir; but the King's guests must be appropriately dressed."

"That's why I came," said Anders. "I want to show the King my cap, my one and only cap, the cap that Mother knitted for me."

"It is a splendid cap," said the guard, "but—"

"But let him in," rang out a lovely voice from behind the guard. "I want to see his splendid cap more clearly."

"It's a one and only cap." Anders couldn't say another word. He realized that he was talking to a princess, who was so beautiful she made him forget everything else in the world. He stood and looked at her, at her pretty pink gown, all ruffles and lace, at her glimmering necklace, at her flowing yellow hair with a little crown perched on top. Then he looked at her smiling face and smiled back.

"Come. Come with me," suggested the Princess. "Our banquet is ready, and you must join us."

Down the garden path they ran, the Princess balancing her little crown on her head and Anders wearing his one and only cap on his head. Up the castle steps they hurried, down the long hall, and into the banquet room, where the guests had already assembled.

Anders couldn't believe his eyes. The table was covered with fruits and cakes and other goodies that he had never seen before. He didn't have time to see it all because, when he and the princess entered, the guests bowed.

The Princess bowed in return. So Anders bowed, too.

The Princess patted the seat of a big gold chair and told Anders to sit on its velvet cushion, next to her. Anders climbed up on the chair. The Princess sat down. All the other guests sat down. But instead of eating they stared and stared at Anders. They began to whisper to each other. They seemed to be talking about his yellow, blue, green, and red stocking cap with the big blue tassel on top.

"You must take off your cap at the banquet table," whispered the Princess. Anders looked around. There was no safe place to lay a cap. The table was full of food. So he kept his cap on his head.

"Please take off your cap now," ordered the Princess gently.

"Oh, no!" cried Anders, clutching his cap. "It's my one and only cap. Mother knitted it just for me. The ladies are wearing caps, but they aren't like mine."

"Look," said the Princess, as she removed her necklace and held it before Anders. "I'll trade my necklace for your cap."

"Thank you," said Anders. "It is a pretty necklace. My mother doesn't have a necklace and I'd like to give her one. But I can't give up my one and only cap." He grabbed his cap and pulled down the edge until it almost covered his eyes.

A roar of laughter rang out across the room. Anders

peeked out from under the edge of his cap. Out of the corner of one eye he saw the King of Sweden standing in the doorway, laughing. Anders knew the man must be the king because the man was wearing a heavy gold crown studded with jewels. Only a king wears a crown like that. The guests stood up, all except Anders.

The King entered the room, strode across the marble floor, and walked to the place where Anders was sitting. The King winked at the Princess and motioned for the guests to be seated.

Then, very seriously, the King took off his golden crown studded with jewels and said, "Little boy, that's a splendid cap you are wearing. Shall we trade hats? I'll give you my crown for awhile and you give me your cap."

"Thank you," said Anders. "My father never had a crown. I know he'd like to wear one." The King moved closer to Anders, holding out the golden crown. Anders grabbed his cap again.

"But I cannot give up my cap," Anders called out, very frightened. "It's a one and only cap. Mother knitted it just for me."

Before the King could say another word, Anders slid off his chair and ran through the palace hall, out the door, down the steps of the castle, along the garden path, out the gate, and down the road that led to home.

All out of breath, Anders burst into the cottage where his mother, father, brothers, and sisters gathered around him.

"My goodness, Anders!" exclaimed his mother. "Where have you been? Why were you gone so long?"

"Everyone wants my cap, even the King," cried Anders.

"The King?" asked his father, mother, brothers, and sisters.

"Yes, even the King," answered Anders. "Everyone wants to trade something for my cap. A boy said he'd trade a jackknife. The Princess said she'd trade her necklace, and the King said he'd trade his crown. But I couldn't give up my cap. It's a one and only cap, And, Mother, you made it just for ME." Anders buried his head, cap and all, in his mother's big apron.

"You were stupid!" said his oldest brother. "You could have sold the crown or the necklace—or even the jackknife—and with the money you could have bought a lot of caps and had money left."

"But this is a one and only cap," cried Anders. "There's not another cap like it in the whole world. Mother made this cap just for ME."

"You are right, Anders," said his mother, as she sat down and gathered Anders into her arms. "There are some things in this world that you cannot buy—not with a crown, not with jewels, not with money. Some things come only with love."

"Like my cap. My one and only cap. The cap you made just for ME," sighed Anders, as he snuggled close in his mother's arms, closed his eyes, and fell asleep. It had been a big day for a boy with a one and only cap, a cap his mother had made just for HIM.

—A Swedish tale retold

Lazy Bones

Let's pretend that you are very, very sleepy. You must get up; but you don't want to get up. So you yawn and yawn. Let's yawn together.

Now let's pretend that you are very, very lazy. You ought to get up; but you don't want to get up. One by one, members of your family try to make you get up. What do you think they might do to get you out of bed? Let's act it out.

Dutchman's Breeches in the following story is a very lazy elf. As you listen to the story, imagine how he felt when his friends played a joke on him.

A Joke on Dutchman's Breeches

Dutchman's Breeches was the laziest elf in all fairy-land. One night, when the moon was shining, Dutchman's Breeches went to bed bright and early. He folded his little breeches neatly beside him, and sank sleepily down into the hummingbird's nest that served him for a cradle. He pulled up his cobweb sheets and soft, green moss blanket, and was soon far away in slumberland.

At the same moment, Johnny-jump-up, Ragged Robin, and Goatsbeard came frolicking through the aspen grove dragging something behind them.

"Ho, ho, ho! Hah, hah, hah! Hee, hee, hee!" they chuckled.

But when they drew near the low-hanging bough of the little bush where Dutchman's cradle was swinging, suddenly they grew very, very still. Quietly they crept close to their wee, sleeping playmate, and set up, square above his head, one of the things they had been dragging. A huge yellow sunflower—that's what it was! Then the three tiny rogues hid behind the leaves, and Johnny-jump-up began to tickle Dutchman's nose with a blade of feathery tufted grass.

Dutchman's Breeches sniffed and wrinkled his nose like a rabbit. Johnny-jump-up went right on tickling. At last Dutchman's Breeches gave a kerchoo! as loud as the tinkle of a raindrop, and opened his eyes square on that big yellow sunflower.

"Why, bless me!" he grumbled. "It's morning. The sun's up, and I'll have to get up, too. Dear me. How I wish I could stay snuggled up in my soft little bed."

Suddenly he threw back his covers and sat up, yawning and stretching, but just as he had one tiny foot over the edge of the hummingbird's nest, his head nodded forward and he fell asleep again. In a twinkling those mischievous elves dragged the sunflower away and hoisted in its place a round, white moonflower. Then they hid again, while one tickled the sleeping fellow on his nose.

Dutchman's Breeches put up one hand and brushed sleepily at the feathery grass. He opened his eyes just far enough to see what was above him.

"Why, bless me!" he cried. "It's night after all. I've bothered myself to get up for nothing! I thought I saw the sun, but I guess— I guess—" And he lay down in his nest and went fast asleep again.

"Ho, ho, ho! Hah, hah, hah! Hee, hee, hee!" chuckled the rogues, and they took down the moonflower and set up the sunflower just as before.

"Twitter, twitter! Chirp, chirp! Cheep, cheep, cheep!" They sang exactly like birds when the morning comes. So Dutchman's Breeches opened one eye.

"Why, there it is again—the sun!" he cried, and he popped up quickly, in great astonishment, and began to pull on his little white breeches. But while he was bent over tugging away, Johnny-jump-up crept up behind him, took down the sunflower, and hoisted the moon-flower.

Soon Dutchman's Breeches sat up on the edge of his nest, yawning, with his little thumbs through his suspenders, but just at that moment he heard the to-whit! to-whoo! of the night owl, and, looking about, he saw the moonflower.

"Oh! Oh! Oh!" he piped. "Is it day or night? Is it night or day? The sun chases away the moon, and the moon chases away the sun! Is it night or day?"

For a moment he pondered, his suspenders still in midair, but he simply could not solve the problem.

"Well!" he said at last. "I guess I'll go to sleep again." And down he plunged into his cozy nest.

Then, snicker and giggle, the three little rascals planted a whole row of sunflowers all about Dutchman's cradle. And they wakened him once again with a sound like the squeak of a squirrel.

"Oh, what's happened to the world?" he wailed. "What's happened to the world? How can any world have a row of suns? Where am I? Where am I?"

Just then Johnny-jump-up, who was hiding behind the biggest sunflower, pulled the stalk back and forth, making that one huge sunflower bow and nod its head.

"The sun's alive," shrieked Dutchman's Breeches. "Oh, deary me, the sun's alive!" And he quickly ducked his head behind his moss blanket and hid.

The elves couldn't hold their laughter a moment longer. They laughed as loudly as elves can. Dutchman's Breeches knew someone was playing a joke on him. Out of his bed he whisked.

"Can't catch us!" piped the three elves, and off they ran. Dutchman's Breeches ran after them.

Around and around the aspen grove he chased them, in and out, among the ferns, up the satiny, white-barked tree trunks, through the lisping, whispering leaves until at last the three rogues disappeared from sight.

Dutchman's Breeches stopped and drew a breath. He

grumbled once. He grunted twice. Then he went back to his cradle, knocked down the row of sunflowers, got back into his cozy nest, pulled up the covers, and fell fast asleep.

—From *Whisk Away on a Sunbeam* by Olive Beaupre Miller, © 1919 by P. F. Volland Co.

More Books to Read

Andrews, Gladys. *Creative Rhythmic Movement for Children.* New York: Prentice-Hall, 1954.

Burger, Isabel B. *Creative Play Acting.* New York: Ronald Press, [1950] 1966.

Carlson, Bernice Wells. *Act It Out.* Nashville: Abingdon Press, 1956.

———. *Play a Part.* Nashville: Abingdon Press, 1970.

Crosscup, Richard. *Children and Dramatics.* New York: Charles Scribner's Sons, 1966.

McCaslin, Nellie. *Creative Dramatics in the Classroom.* New York: David McKay Company, 1968.

Olfson, Lewy. *You Can Act.* New York: Sterling Publishing Company, [1965] 1971.

Siks, Geraldine Brain. *Creative Dramatics: An Art for Children.* New York: Harper & Row, 1960.

Ward, Winifred. *Playmaking with Children from Kindergarten Through Junior High School.* 2nd ed. New York: Appleton-Century-Crofts, 1957.

Index